# Religious Knowledge for Pri
## Grade 1
## Workbook

By Cynthia Smith

# Table of Contents

God made the world.
Genesis 1—2:25

What is something God made that you are glad for?

Lesson: 1

The Nature of God
## The Beginning

In the beginning, God created the heavens and the earth. On the first day, God created day and night. On the second day, God created the sky. There were evening and morning on the second day. On the third day, God created land and the seas. God put plants on the land. On the fourth day, God created the sun, moon, and stars. On the fifth day, God created sea animals, and he created birds to fly in the air. On the sixth day, God created land animals. God also created man and woman in His own likeness. God told them to be fruitful and increase in numbers. God gave the man the responsibility of ruling over all the animals. On the seventh day, God rested. God made the seventh day holy.

Date: _____

Use the numbers in the box and write it under the correct picture to show the day when God created it.

1 2 3 4 5 6 7

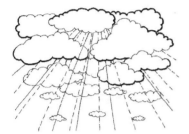

day and night

_____

God made a man

_____

_____

fish and birds

_____

plants on the land

_____

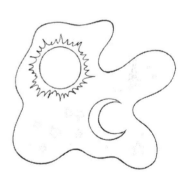

sun and moon

_____

Lesson: 2

## The Nature of God
# Adam and Eve

Adam lived in a beautiful garden called Eden. Here, God gave him everything he needed – food and water. God also told Adam to look after the garden.

**What was the name of the place where Adam lived?**
**The G __ __ __ __ __ of**
**E __ __ __**

Have you ever been left on your own? It is not always nice being all alone.
God didn't want Adam to be alone.

Adam was surrounded by many beautiful animals, birds, trees and plants, but God knew he needed someone special to share his life in the garden.

God put Adam into a deep sleep, and while he was asleep, He made the first woman called Eve.

Adam was no longer alone. He now had someone who would be his wife and companion as he looked after the garden in which God had put him.

**Colour and learn the verse below.**

"The earth is the Lord's and everything in it."

Lesson: 3

## The Nature of God
# Baby Jesus is Born

Mary and Joseph had to make the long journey from Nazareth to Bethlehem. This was because of an order from the Roman Emperor.

Bethlehem was very crowded but at last, they found somewhere to stay. It was the place in which animals were kept. Here Jesus was born, and Mary wrapped Him up in some strips of cloth. She put Him in a manger in which the animals' food was usually put.

**Circle the correct answers.**

Mary and Joseph were only able to find room in:
**an inn**           **a palace**           **a hospital**           **an animal shed**

Jesus was placed in:
**a bed**                    **a manger**                    **a crib**

Hundreds of babies are born every day around the world, but there never has been a baby like this. This Baby is the Son of God!

This Christmas, remember to thank God for His great love in sending His own Son into this world to be our Saviour.

Lesson: 4

## The Nature of God
## **The Lost Sheep**

Have you ever been lost? If so, you will know how marvelous it is when someone finds you and takes you home.  Jesus told a story about a shepherd who had 100 sheep and one sheep became lost.  The shepherd left all the other sheep and went to look for the lost one.  He wasn't happy until he found it. When, at last, he found the sheep, he put it on his shoulders. Gladly, he carried it home.

**Fill in the missing numbers and words.**

The shepherd had __ __ __ sheep. He lost o __ __ sheep.

The shepherd f __ __ __ __ the l __ __ __ sheep.

The Bible says we are like sheep which are lost. The Lord Jesus is the Good Shepherd, who wants to find us and care for us. He gave His life for us - that's how much He cares.

**Colour and learn these words.   Jesus said,**

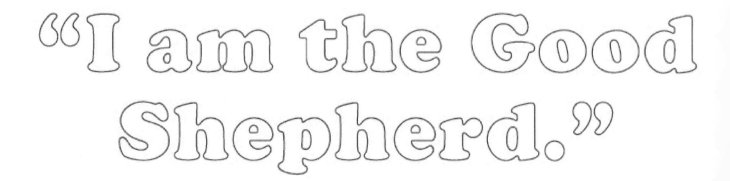

"I am the Good Shepherd."

Lesson: 5

## The Nature of God
# The Lost Son

Another story Jesus told was about a son who was tired of living at home. He asked his father to give him some money. His father gave it to him and then he left home. He went to a faraway land.

At first, he had a great time. He spent his money foolishly. When it was all spent, his many new friends didn't want to know him anymore. Then there was a famine and food was very hard to find. The only job he could get was looking after pigs.

When he realized how foolish he had been, he decided to go home and say he was sorry. His father saw him coming, ran to meet him and welcomed him home. His father forgave him and held a big party to show how pleased he was to have his son home.

**Check the correct answer.**

His father told him off. _____

His father forgave him. _____

His father chased him away. _____

God is waiting for us to say we are sorry for doing wrong things. He is willing to forgive us and to receive us into His family.

Lesson: 6

# Honoring God

The word "worship" means to respect, honour, and worship a divine being.  It is also a special service or ceremony.  Human beings were made to worship and praise their creator, God.  This is their purpose or reason for being alive.  Psalm 95:6 states that we should worship, bow down, and kneel before the Lord our Maker.

We can worship God through song, dance, praise, and playing of musical instruments.  Worship can also be done in quiet reverence in prayer.

1. Tell one thing we do when we worship. [1] _____.

2. Worship means **r** ___ ___ ___ ___ ___ ___

3. We were made to worship our

c ____ ___ ___ ___ ___ ___ ___

4. We worship God in **p** ____ ____ __ __ ____ ____.

Lesson: 7

## Discovering my Identify

There are many things that make each person different. For example, the colour of his/her hair, eyes and skin. Individuals also have different likes and dislikes.

Each person is a unique and special being. Psalm 139:14 states, "I will praise you for I am fearfully and wonderfully made; marvelous are thy works and that my soul knoweth right well." God did not make any mistakes in His design.

Each individual has special abilities or gifts. For example singing, dancing, speaking or writing. These are also called talents at church, at home, and at school.

A. List two things that you do well. [2]

1. _____

2. _____

Lesson: 8

Serving Others
# A Voice in the Night

When Samuel was very young, his mother took him to Shiloh to visit Eli, the priest, in the House of the Lord. Hannah reminded Eli about her earlier visit and about her prayer to God. Again, she gave thanks to God. She kept her promise to God, by leaving Samuel with Eli, so that he could serve God. We should never forget to thank God when He answers our prayers. One night, while Eli and Samuel were asleep, the Lord called Samuel by name. At first, Samuel thought it was Eli calling him, so he ran to Eli. Eventually, Eli realized that it was the Lord who was calling Samuel. So Eli told Samuel that if he was called again, he was to say, "Speak, Lord, for your servant is listening."

**1. Put the following pictures in their correct order by labelling them 1 to 5. [5]**

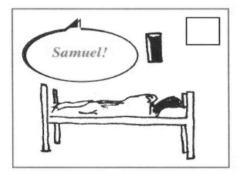 

**2. How many times did Samuel go to Eli? Circle the correct answer.  [1]**

4 times          2 times          5 times          3 times

**Write YES or NO after the following sentences:- [3]**

3. Samuel slept soundly through the night. _____

4. Eli realized after the third time that the Lord was speaking to Samuel. ___

5. Samuel did not know the Lord. _____

6. Eli's sons also heard the Lord speaking. _____

Serving Others
## Naaman is healed

Naaman was a great army commander.  He was a brave soldier, but he had a problem.  He had a terrible skin disease called leprosy. One day Naaman's wife said, "My servant told me you should go see the prophet, Elisha. He can heal you." Naaman reached Elisha's home. Elisha sent out a man with this message. "Dunk yourself in the Jordan River seven time. Then you will be healed."

At first, Naaman thought it was a silly idea. But his servants said, "Please go.  This is not a hard thing to do."  So Naaman dunked himself in the Jordan River seven times.  When he was done, Naaman's skin disease was gone! Naaman was so excited that he ran to thank Elisha for curing him.  Naaman said, "Israel's God is the only true God!"

Fill in the blanks.

1. Naaman was a brave _____ .

2. His sickness was _____ .

3. He had to dunk in the river _____ times.

4. He had to go to the _____ River.

## Overcoming Obstacles
# David and Goliath

Goliath was a giant in the Philistine army. The Philistines did not trust in God. The Israelites and the Philistines were at war. The Israelites did trust in God. Many times in the past God had helped them to win battles when they trusted Him. Every day Goliath shouted, "Choose one of your men to fight me. If he wins and kills me, we will be your slaves, but if I win and kill him, you will be our slaves." Every time the Israelites heard Goliath shouting, they were afraid. They forgot that God would help them.

**What was the name of the giant? G __ __ __ __ __ __**

**Put a circle around the word that describes how the Israelites felt when they heard Goliath.**

**afraid        happy        sad**

One day, David's father sent him to the battle to see how his brothers were doing.
While he was there, he heard Goliath shouting and saw how frightened the people were.

"King Saul has promised to give a big reward to the man who kills him," they said.
God had promised to look after the Israelites if they trusted in Him. David trusted God and told everyone that the Lord could beat Goliath.
David told Saul what he had done. He knew that the Lord would help him to fight Goliath.

Saul gave David his armour, but it was too big for him. David took five stones from the brook and his sling. When Goliath saw David, he laughed. He thought he would easily kill David. David trusted in God to help him. He put one stone in his sling, and the stone hit the giant on the forehead. Goliath fell to the ground. David ran and took Goliath's sword and killed him. David was able to kill Goliath because he trusted in God.

**Colour the words that show who David trusted in.**

Lesson: 11

Overcoming Obstacles
# Samson

Samson fell in love with a woman named Delilah. The Philistines were happy to hear this. "Find out the secret of Samson's strength and then we can tie him up," the Philistines said, "We will give you silver if you do." Samson tricked Delilah by telling her three different ways he could be tied up. Each time he was tied up, though, he was able to break free. Delilah cried because Samson had made a fool of her. "If you love me, why won't you tell me the secret of your strength?" said Delilah.

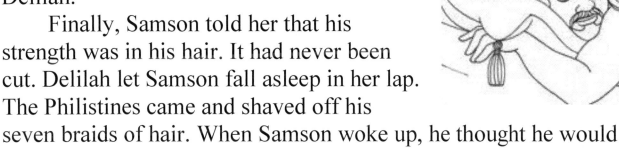

   Finally, Samson told her that his strength was in his hair. It had never been cut. Delilah let Samson fall asleep in her lap. The Philistines came and shaved off his seven braids of hair. When Samson woke up, he thought he would have his strength still. Samson did not know that the Lord had left him.

Complete the blanks.

1. Samson fell in love with _____.

2. Samson gave _____ ways he could be tied up.

3. Samson strength was in his _____.

4. Samson fell a ___  ___  ____  ____  ____  _____.

Celebrating Thanksgiving
# Hanna's Prayer

Elkanah had two wives. One was called Hannah and the other Peninnah. Peninnah had several children and often laughed at Hannah, and was unkind to her because Hannah had no children.

Each year Elkanah and his family visited Shiloh, to worship the Lord.
On one visit, Hannah was very upset because of the unkind words Peninnah had said.

After their meal, Hannah decided to go and pray to God. As Hannah was praying, Eli, the priest, sat by the door watching her. She cried, as she told the Lord her problem. She asked God to give her a baby boy and promised he would always serve the Lord.

**Who was watching Hannah pray? E __ __**

Even though her lips were moving, Eli heard no words. He thought she was drunk. She was speaking to God in her heart!  Hannah quickly told Eli that she wasn't drunk, only very sad and upset. She explained how she had been praying to the Lord. Eli replied,

**"Go home, and don't be upset and**

**what you have asked Him for."**

Sometime later, Hannah gave birth to a baby boy. God answered her prayer!

Lesson: 13

Celebrating Thanksgiving
## The Ten Lepers

One day as Jesus was going into a village, He was met by ten men who had leprosy. They had a horrible skin disease, which meant they could not live at home. Hardly anyone ever got better from leprosy.

When they saw Jesus, they shouted, "Jesus, Master, have mercy on us!" Jesus told them to go and show themselves to the priests. At once they obeyed. As they went to find the priests the miracle happened. All ten men were healed!

They all saw the wonderful change that had taken place, but sadly, only one of them went back to thank the Lord Jesus. When Jesus saw him, He asked, "Where are the others?" Jesus praised the man for coming back to thank Him. This man was not from the same country as Jesus and the other nine men. He was a Samaritan. He was more thankful than his nine friends.

**Colour the correct number to answer these questions.**
How many men were healed?

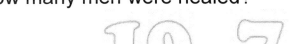

How many returned to say, "Thank You"?

We, too, must 'trust and obey' the Lord Jesus and say, "Thank You" to Him for His love, and all that He has done for us.

Lesson: 14

Celebrating Christmas

# The Angel Visited Mary

The angel Gabriel had first told Zechariah and Elizabeth that they would have a son. Now the angel was making a special visit to Mary. Mary was told that she, too, would have a son and that His name was to be Jesus.

**What was the name of the mother of Jesus? [1]**

_____

Mary's Son is much greater than the son of Zechariah and Elizabeth, for He is the Son of God.

Mary was not sure how this great event could happen. The angel told her all would be well.

**Colour what the angel said to Mary.**

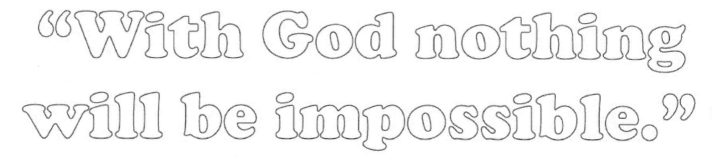

"With God nothing will be impossible."

Mary believed all the angel said. How unlike Zechariah who didn't believe!  Mary was willing to accept God's plan and become the mother of this very special Baby. We, too, need to trust God fully.
The birth of the Lord Jesus was one of the greatest miracles that ever happened!

Lesson: 15

Celebrating Christmas
# The Shepherd and the Wise men

When Jesus was born, an angel first told some shepherds about His birth.

**Colour the picture and the three special names the angel used for Jesus. "Unto you is born this day in the city of David a**

Saviour

who is

Christ

the

Lord."

The shepherds were told that the Baby had been born in Bethlehem, and they would find Him wrapped in cloths and lying in a manger.

A new star had appeared in the sky. Wise Men in the east knew that this was a sign of the birth of a new King. They travelled to Jerusalem wanting to find the Child so they could worship Him. This news didn't please Herod. He was king and he did not want anyone else to take his place!

**What were the Wise Men going to do when they found the Child? Cross out the wrong answer.**

kill Him            worship Him

Herod did not know where the Child was, so he asked some of his advisors if they knew where the Child was to be born. They said He was to be born in

Bethlehem.

Soon the Wise Men arrived at Bethlehem and found the house where Jesus, Joseph and Mary were staying. When they saw Jesus, they worshiped Him. The Wise Men had brought three gifts for Jesus - gold, frankincense and myrrh.

## Choices
### The Sneaky Snake

God had told Adam and Eve that they could eat the fruit from every tree in the garden except one. One day, God's enemy, Satan, disguised as a snake, came into the garden.

**Who is God's enemy? [1] S __ __ __ __**

The Sneaky Snake told Eve that if she ate fruit from that tree, she would be as clever as God! She then disobeyed God and took some of the fruit. She gave some to Adam and they both ate it.

God sent Adam and Eve out of the garden. Their sin had spoiled God's creation and ruined their friendship with God.

God promised that one day Satan would be destroyed, and a way back to Him would be possible. This all happened when the Lord Jesus came into the world and died on the cross for sinners.

The Lord Jesus Christ took the punishment for our sins. We can be forgiven when we put

our trust in Him.

**Colour the words above.**

Lesson: 17

Growing with Value

## Jesus Feeds Five Thousand

I'm sure you like to go for a picnic or barbeque. It's good fun to eat outside on a warm day.

This story is about a very large picnic. Many people had come to listen to the Lord Jesus. They had been away from home for a long time and were getting very hungry. There was nowhere to buy any food.

Andrew, one of Jesus' helpers, found out that a boy in the crowd had a lunch of five small loaves and two fish. It was just enough for the boy himself, but he gave it all to Andrew who brought it to Jesus.

**Join the dots to see what was in the lunch, and then colour the picture.**

**Who brought the lunch to Jesus?**

A __ __ __ __ __

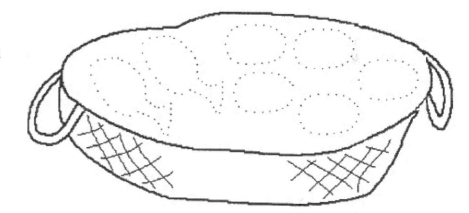

Jesus told the people to sit down and then He gave thanks to God for the food.
After that, Jesus' helpers started to pass the bread and fish around. There was so much food that every single person had enough to eat! The Lord Jesus was able to make food for everyone because He is the Son of God.

Lesson: 18

Growing in Value
## Noah's Ark

Noah was a good man who obeyed God. Everyone else in the world had become bad.

God told Noah that He was going to send a flood to destroy all living things. He told Noah to build a big boat (known as Noah's Ark).

God sent two of each kind of bird and animal to Noah to load in the ark. He sent more than two of some of the animals. Noah also loaded his three sons, their wives, and his own wife. It began to rain. God closed the door.

It rained for 40 days and 40 nights. Everything on earth was under water. Everyone on earth died, but Noah and his family were safe and dry.

When the rain stopped and the land dried, God sent a rainbow as a sign of the promise that He would never again destroy the earth with water.

1. The rain lasted for _____ days and _____ nights.

2. There were _____ of each kinds of animals in the ark.

3. How many people were in the ark? _____

4. Who built the ark? _____

Growing in Value
## A Hole in the Roof

When the crowd heard that Jesus had come home, they crowded

inside the house. There was no room left, not even outside the door. Jesus preached the word of God to the crowd. Four men carried a paralytic man to see Jesus. Since they could not get to Jesus because of the crowd, they made an opening in the roof and lowered the man to Jesus. When Jesus saw their faith, he said the paralytic, "Son, your sins are forgiven." Jesus wanted to show the teachers that he had the authority to forgive sins. So Jesus told the paralytic man, "Get up, take your mat and go home."

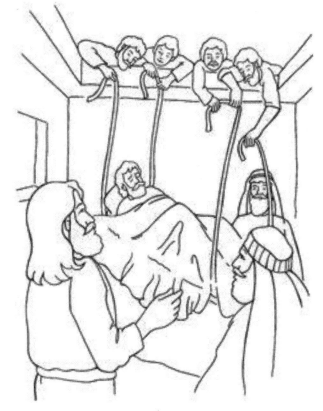

1. How many of the man's friend took him to see Jesus? _____
2. Friends let the man down through the ____ ____ ____ ____.
3. Colour the words Jesus said to the man.

# "your sins are forgiven."

Lesson: 21

Growing in Value
## Lazarus Lives Again

It was a very sad time for Mary and Martha. Their brother **Lazarus** had died. His body was wrapped in pieces of cloth and put in a cave with a big stone across the front.

Four days after Lazarus was buried, Jesus came to visit Mary and Martha. He felt very sorry for His friends. He saw the place where Lazarus was buried, and as He thought about His friend, He **cried** too.

Then Jesus did a very strange thing. He asked some of the people at the tomb to take away the stone. Next, He called out in a loud voice, **"Lazarus, come out!"** Before everyone's eyes, Lazarus walked out, still wrapped in the pieces of cloth.

Jesus had the power to give life back to Lazarus. Mary and Martha knew now how very special their Friend, Jesus, was!

**Whom did Jesus bring back to life?**

L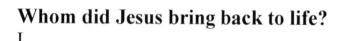

Colour the picture and the words that Jesus said.

# "I am the resurrection and the life."

Lesson: 22

Growing in Value
## Jesus Heal a Blind Beggar

A blind man was sitting at the edge of the road. He was begging, hoping that a kind person would give him some money.

One day there were many people walking past. Something special was happening. Then someone told the blind man that Jesus was coming.

How excited he was! He knew that Jesus could help him see! So he started to shout Jesus' name as loudly as he could. Jesus heard him and called him over.

**Who was coming?  J \_\_\_\_ \_\_\_\_ \_\_\_\_ \_\_\_\_**

**The man knew that Jesus could make him s \_\_\_\_ \_\_\_\_ .**

The man told Jesus that he wanted to see. The Lord Jesus was pleased that the man trusted in Him. Jesus spoke to him again, and suddenly he could see! Joyfully, he followed the Lord Jesus down the road, thanking God for what had happened.

Growing in Value
# Two Miracles

Jairus was a worried man. His little girl was very, very ill. No doctor could make her better. Then Jairus decided to ask Jesus for help. He knew that Jesus could heal people.

Soon Jairus found Jesus. They were walking back to Jairus' house when some men came and told them that it was too late. The girl was dead! There was no point in Jesus coming.

**To whom did Jairus go for help? J __ __ __ __**

But Jesus did not allow Jairus to go home alone. He told him not to be afraid.

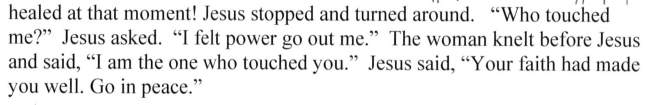

A large crowd followed Jesus as he walked to Jairus' house.  As they were going a woman pushed through the crowd toward Jesus.  She had been sick for twelve years.  The woman believed that Jesus could heal her.  She knew if she just touch his clothes.  She will be healed.

The moment she touched Jesus, she reached out and touched him.  She was healed at that moment! Jesus stopped and turned around.   "Who touched me?" Jesus asked. "I felt power go out me."  The woman knelt before Jesus and said, "I am the one who touched you."  Jesus said, "Your faith had made you well. Go in peace."

When Jesus arrived at Jairus' house, they found many people crying. Then Jesus took Jairus and the girl's mother and Peter, James and John into the girl's room.  Jesus took the girl by the hand and told her to get up. At once, she got up and walked around!

**Fill in the missing words.**

The girl was **d** __ __ __ but Jesus brought her back to **l** __ __ __.

Lesson: 24

Growing with Value
## Kindness

Kindness is the act or quality of being kind: being thoughtful to others and showing understanding to their feelings. When we are kind to others, we show obedience to God's Word. We also make people happy when we are kind.

Ephesians 4:32 states that we should "be kind to each other, tenderhearted, forgiving one another, even as God for Jesus' sake forgiving us. Kindness is part of the Fruit of the Spirit.

I can follow Jesus by sharing.

Some acts of kindness we can perform are opening the door for someone, sharing our lunch, using nice words, and other things.

1. ___ ___ ___ ___ ___ ___ ___ ____ is the act of being kind.

2. We show _____ to God when we are kind.

3. What do we do when we are kind? Colour the word.

## Caring for God's Creation
# Adam and Eve

Adam lived in a beautiful garden called Eden. Here, God gave him everything he needed – food and water. God also told Adam to look after the garden.

**What was the name of the place where Adam lived?**

**The G __ __ __ __ __ of E __ __ __**

God didn't want Adam to be alone. Adam was surrounded by many beautiful animals, birds, trees and plants, but God knew he needed someone special to share his life in the garden.

God put Adam into a deep sleep, and while he was asleep, He made the first woman called Eve.

Adam was no longer alone. He now had someone who would be his wife and companion as he looked after the garden in which God had put him.

**Colour and learn the verse below.**

"The earth is the Lord's and everything in it."

Rights/Responsibility
# The Ten Commandments

The Israelites came to a big mountain called **Sinai.** Moses went up the mountain. There was a lot of thunder and lightning, as well as thick cloud and fire. It was very frightening.

**Write on the mountain its name**.

But the most wonderful thing that happened was that God met Moses there. God gave him His laws or rules. These rules were to help the Israelites understand how God expected them to behave. We usually call these laws 'The Ten Commandments'.

When we have a very important message to pass on to someone, we always write it down. That's what God did! He wrote His rules on two big stones and gave them to Moses.

God's laws said that they were to love God more than anything else and that they were to love each other.

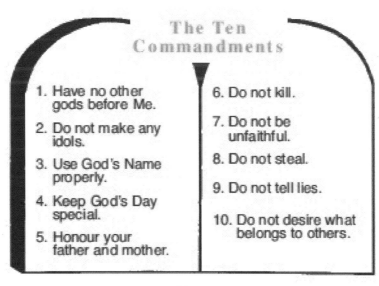

The Ten Commandments

1. Have no other gods before Me.
2. Do not make any idols.
3. Use God's Name properly.
4. Keep God's Day special.
5. Honour your father and mother.
6. Do not kill.
7. Do not be unfaithful.
8. Do not steal.
9. Do not tell lies.
10. Do not desire what belongs to others.

Love and/or forgiveness

## Love

**Love** is defined as a strong **affection** for another person. Some everyday symbols that can be used to explain the ideas of love are a heart, ring, and circle.

---

Love is caring and patience. Love is taking care of things and being polite. Love is a lot of things. There are so many ways to show love.

Lauren loved her class. She especially loved her classroom pet, Benny, the Hamster. Every day Lauren said hello to Benny. She was the classroom pet helper. She fed Benny, cleaned his cage, and gave him water. Lauren loved and cared for Benny, the Hamster.

Jon loved his class. He loved his teacher because she taught him so much. He loved his classroom because it had lots of cool stuff in it. He loved his classmates because they were kind, helpful, and fun. He always did his best to keep his class happy and clean. That was how he showed his love for his class. How do you show love?

Andrew Frinkle

We love you!

Date: _____

1. What kind of class pet is in Lauren's class?
A fish          B mouse          C lizard          D hamster

2. Who takes care of Benny, the Hamster?
A Lois          B Lauren          C Lana          D Lara

3. Lauren loved and cared for _____ the hamster.
A Bratty          B Benny          C Bonnie          D Bunny

4. Jon loved his class.
A True          B False

5. I can show love by _____

Celebrating Easter
# The True King

Jesus and his disciples went to Jerusalem for the Passover Feast. Jesus told two disciples to bring him a donkey. He told them where to find it. Jesus rode the donkey into Jerusalem. A big crowd welcomed him. People waved palm branches and put them on the road in front of Jesus. The shouted, "Hosanna! Hosanna! Blessed is the king of Israel!" The leaders in Jerusalem did not like Jesus. They saw how many people were following him, and they were angry about it. They were jealous.

Fill in the blanks.

1. The Passover was at J___ ___ ___ ___ ___ ___ ___ ___.

2. Jesus rode on a _____.

3. The people shouted _____!

Celebrating Easter
## Jesus is Arrested and Crucified

The time was coming when the Lord Jesus would be put to death. One of His disciples, called **Judas,** went to Jesus' enemies. He promised to lead them to where Jesus would be so that they could arrest Him. For helping them, the chief priests gave Judas **30 silver** coins.

**Fill in the missing letters.**

The c _ _ _ f  p r i _ _ _ _ _  g a v e  J _ _ _ _ s  m o n e y.

Not long after that, the Lord Jesus was praying in a garden called **Gethsemane**. As He finished praying, Judas arrived, leading a crowd of men. They were carrying swords and sticks. Judas greeted Jesus with a **kiss,** and just then the crowd seized Him. The disciples, who had been with Jesus, ran off, and He was led away as a prisoner.

**Colour the words and pictures. The Lord Jesus was arrested in the**

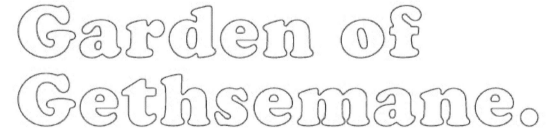

Garden of Gethsemane.

After being arrested, the Lord Jesus was tried by a Roman Governor called **Pontius Pilate**. He felt sure that Jesus had not done anything wrong, and he wanted to set Him free. The Jews, however, wanted **Barabbas**, who was a very popular prisoner, set free. They demanded that Jesus should die. Pilate let the Jews have their way. Barabbas was freed, and the Lord Jesus was sentenced to be put on a cross. Before they crucified Him, the soldiers treated Him very badly. They made **fun** of Him by dressing Him in a **scarlet robe** and putting a **crown of thorns** on His head. They also **spat** on Him and hit Him. Then they nailed Him to a cross.

Fill in the missing letters.

A s c _ _ _ _ t r _ _ e.

A c r _ _ _ _ of t _ _ _ n s.

The Bible tells us He was dying for our sins. There was no other way we could be forgiven and made ready for Heaven!

Celebrating Easter
### Jesus is Risen

The Lord Jesus died on the cross. That very evening, a rich man called Joseph asked Pilate for His body. He wanted to bury Him. Pilate let him have Jesus' body.

**Underline the RIGHT word.**

The Lord Jesus **fainted / died** on the cross.

Joseph was a **rich / poor** man.

Joseph wanted to **bury / burn** Jesus' body.

As soon as Joseph got the body, he wrapped it in clean linen cloth. He put it in a new tomb which belonged to him.
A big stone was rolled across
the entrance of the tomb.

**Colour the picture of Joseph at the tomb.**

Three days later, the Lord
Jesus rose from the dead.
Only God could do such a
wonderful thing! Today the
Lord Jesus is a living Saviour.
He is able to save all who trust Him.

**Colour these words from the Bible.**

"He is risen!"

As Jesus had predicted, He was betrayed. For thirty pieces of silver, Judas Iscariot, an apostle, conspired with the chief priests to betray Him.

Lesson: 31

Respect
**What Do You Sand For**

Respect is showing appreciation and listening to others. It is recognizing the good in others and honoring what they do for us. There are many ways to show respect. Dean really liked Mr. Matthews' class. Mr. Matthews knew a LOT about science. Dean always tried to stump Mr. Matthews with hard questions, but he hadn't confused his teacher yet! He would keep trying. He really appreciated how Mr. Matthews answered his questions, even after class. Gina loved figure skating. Part of it was because she had the best coach ever! Gina's coach was great at skating, so she understood exactly what Gina went through as she learned. Gina respected her coach's abilities and advice. How do you show respect?

www.coloring-pages-kids.com

1. What class does Mr. Matthews teach?
A science        B math        C music        D gym

2. Who really likes Mr. Matthews' class?
(a) Don        (b) Dean        (c) Dina        (d) Dylan

3. Gina _____ figure skating.
A hated        B loved        C watched        D followed

4. Gina didn't like how her coach taught her.
A True        B False

5. I can show respect by

Lesson: 32

## Friendship
### Best Friends

King Saul was so jealous of David that he tried to kill him. David had to hide to be safe.

David's best friend was Jonathan, King Saul's son. Jonathan was able to warn David of his danger. Sometimes David and Jonathan would meet secretly, and have a talk about Saul's wicked plans.

**Who wanted to kill David?**

S _ _ _

**Who was David's best friend?**

J _ _ _ _ _ _ _

How thankful David was to have someone who really loved him! Jonathan was a true
friend. He helped to save David's life. The Bible tells us that Jonathan loved David,

# as much as he loved himself.

**Colour the letters.**

Do you know that the Lord Jesus loves you and that He wants to be your Friend? He loves you so much that He died for you! Do trust Him today!

Celebrating Pentecost
## Jesus Goes to Heaven

When Jesus had risen from the dead, the disciples had spent some wonderful times with the Lord Jesus. Now they understood more about why He had died. It was now over six weeks since the Lord Jesus had risen. He took the eleven disciples to a hill called the **Mount of Olives**. He explained to them that the time had come for Him to go back to Heaven. They would not be left alone because soon a special Helper, the Holy Spirit, would come upon them.

**Write the name of the hill.**  M _ _ _ _    o _    O _ _ _ _ _ .

**Draw Jesus and the correct number of disciples standing on the hill.** (*The first two have been done for you.*)

**Who was the special Helper who would come?**

T _ _    H _ _ _    S _ _ _ _ _ _

As Jesus was talking to His disciples, He was suddenly lifted up off the ground. Soon a cloud hid Him from their view. The disciples stood staring into the sky. Two angels appeared beside them.
"Why are you standing looking into the sky?" the angel asked.
"This same Jesus will come back again."

Celebrating Pentecost
## The Holy Spirit Comes

Thousands of people went to Jerusalem to celebrate a Jewish holiday called Pentecost. They came from many countries and spoke many different languages. Jesus' disciples were staying there. They were praying together. Suddenly, a noise filled the room. It sounded like a strong wind blowing. The Holy Spirit appeared as tongues of fire on each of them. They started talking in languages they did not know. The people in Jerusalem heard the noise and came to see what was happening. The crowd was amazed and asked, "How are you able to speak our language?" Peter said, "The prophets told us this would happen. Then Peter told them about God's plan. "God sent Jesus to save everyone from the bad things we have done."

The people asked, "What should we do?" Peter replied, "Ask Jesus to forgive you for your sins and be baptized in the name of Jesus Christ." On that day, 3000 people believed in Jesus. The disciples baptized all of them.

Fill in the blanks.

1. People when to _____ for the Passover feast.

2. The _____ _____ came like fire.

3. People spoke in many _____.

4. _____ people believed in Jesus.

# Work Cited

Department of Education. (1997). *Commonwealth of The Bahamas, Ministry of Education Religious Studies Curriculum Guideline*s (Draft, Grade Levels 1, 2, 3)

Henley. K, and Davis, D. (2005). *The Beginner's Bible Timeless Bible Stories*, Mission city press

http://www.bible-n-more.com/pbs-lessons/bibletime-lessons/

Made in United States
Orlando, FL
03 September 2022

21964670R00026